To Singapore and Beyond

A brief history of the 4th, 5th and 6th Battalions, Royal Norfolk Regiment, from 1939 to 1945

Compiled by Neil Storey

This book is dedicated to:

— and —

The memory of
5770986
L/SGT. OSWALD JAMES GRIFFIN
'C' Company, 5th Battalion,
Royal Norfolk Regiment.
Killed in action, Alexandra Hospital,
Singapore, February 13th 1942

My dear friend
5776790
PTE. IVOR CHARLES SELF
'HQ' Company, 5th Battalion,
Royal Norfolk Regiment,
who returned and has
'kept going the spirit'.

Published by:
HOLYBOY PUBLICATIONS
(N. Storey)
91 Clifton Street,
Norwich,
Norfolk NR2 4NE

First Impression 1992

© Neil Storey 1992

ISBN 0 9520132 0 7

All rights reserved. No part of this publication may be reproduced, stored in a retrieval system or transmitted in any form or by any means, elec tronic, mechanical, photocopying, recording, or otherwise, without prior permission of the publisher.

Printed by:
COLOURPRINT
The Drift,
Fakenham,
Norfolk NR21 8EE

Acknowledgements

I would like to thank all the people who, along the years, have inspired and made this book possible, especially: Vic Brown, The Imperial War Museum, Major William Reeve, Lieutenant Colonel Alan Cubitt, Major Tom Eaton, OBE, TD, DL, Major Harry Schulman, MBE, TD, Major Monty Smyth, MBE, Ivor Self, Bob Driver, Harry Browne, Bertie Perkins, Keith Skipper, the Trustees of the Royal Norfolk Regimental Museum, Kate Thaxton and all my pals in FEPOW.

Front cover illustration:
His Majesty King George VI, accompanied by Lieut. Col. J. H. Jewson, MC, TD, inspects members of the 4th Battalion, Royal Norfolk Regiment, at Gorleston, 23rd August 1940

18th DIVISION

Forword

We, the undersigned officers who served respectively in the 4th, 5th and 6th (Territorial) Battalions of the Royal Norfolk Regiment warmly commend "To Singapore and Beyond", the brief history of the Battalions in which we served 1939 to 1945.

This book, produced to mark the 50th anniversary of the Fall of Singapore, records for veterans and future generations the spirit and comradeship which enabled men to endure and survive the many hardships and cruelties of three and a half years as prisoners of war of the Japanese.

CAPTAIN T. C. EATON, OBE, TD, DL
EX-4TH BATTALION THE ROYAL NORFOLK REGIMENT
PRESIDENT OF THE NORWICH FELLOWSHIP OF EX-POW (FAR EAST)

MAJOR H. E. SCHULMAN, MBE, TD
EX-5TH BATTALION THE ROYAL NORFOLK REGIMENT
PRESIDENT OF FAKENHAM FEPOW

LIEUT. COL. A. B. CUBITT
LAST BC 6TH BATTALION THE ROYAL NORFOLK REGIMENT

EXPANSION OF THE
TERRITORIAL ARMY

TO MEN OF NORFOLK

Owing to wanton aggression and attempts at world domination by certain powers the peace of the whole world and the most sacred traditions of all the democracies are threatened. Therefore, we as a nation must be ready to meet and answer any such aggression.

The Government has decided that an immediate expansion of the Territorial Army shall be carried out. This means that all Field Force Units of the Territorial Army in the County of Norfolk, after being brought up to their full establishment, will have to be doubled again in numbers.

We must be prepared. REMEMBER ENGLAND EXPECTS EVERY MAN TO DO HIS DUTY and that the personal sacrifice called for is a small price to pay as an insurance for world peace and for the safety of all we hold dear in this life.

We MUST now prove to the world that our VOLUNTARY SYSTEM of which we are justly proud is a reality, not a mere phrase, by the manhood of the nation coming forward and giving their services in the armed forces of the nation.

The Whole World Awaits Your Answer

We earnestly appeal to you, Men of Norfolk, to join one of the undermentioned Territorial Army Units.

Please apply AT ONCE either personally or by letter or telephone to any of the following addresses

UNIT	ADDRESS	Tel. No.	UNIT	ADDRESS	Tel. No.
219th Anti-Tank Battery Headquarters and 220th Anti-Tank Battery	Drill Hall, Cattle Market, Norwich	[Norwich 1242]	H.Q. Company	Drill Hall, Wellesley Street King's Lynn	
4th Bn. The Royal Norfolk Regt.	,, ,, Spinners Lane, Swaffham	[Swaffham 244]	" B " Company	,, ,, Next to the Church Lane Fakenham	
Bn. H.Q. and "A" Coy.	,, ,, Chapel Field Rd., Norwich	[Norwich 656]	" C " Company	,, ,, Pound Lane, Aylsham	[Aylsham 212]
" B " Company	,, ,, Queens Rd. Attleborough	[Attleborough 2140]	" D " Company	,, ,, Dersingham	
" C " Company	,, ,, Harleston	[Harleston 44]	250th. Field Company R. E.	,, ,, Cattle Market, Norwich	
" D " Company	,, ,, Drill Hall, York Road Great Yarmouth		183rd. (E. A.) Field Ambulance	,, ,, No. 2, Hiliary Avenue, Plumstead Rd. Norwich	
5th Bn. The Royal Norfolk Regt. Bn. H.Q. and H.Q. Coy.	,, ,, Norwich Rd., E. Dereham		41st. A.A. Divisional R.A.O.C. Workshop Company	22, Tombland, Norwich	

GOD SAVE THE KING

Introduction

This book has come about for a number of reasons. I have always been interested in the County of Norfolk, where my family has lived for hundreds of years, and the Royal Norfolk Regiment in which many of my ancestors have served in its various forms.

During the Fall of Singapore my great-uncle was, as the official forms said: "Missing in Action". My great-grandparents lived in hope for years for the return of their son. My grandmother related the story of how the family never really knew what happened to her brother Oswald.

I set out with an open mind to try and ascertain what really happened, all I knew he was a Territorial soldier and roughly when and where he had served with the Royal Norfolk Regiment. Quite by chance I happened to see an advert in the paper for "A Far Eastern War Exhibition, telling the real story of the war and life in Japanese prisoner of war camps", held at Cromer church hall. I went along. Talking to Vic Brown, who had put on the exhibition, and members of the Far Eastern Prisoners of War (FEPOW) group, some of whom knew Oswald, and one veteran knew more or less what had happened to him. The honesty and manner which these gentlemen talked to me, almost as if they had known me for years, the time they had for me, obvious was the great comradeship and care they have for their mates who were still around and those like me who had lost family. They realised how much I cared about my great-uncle, who I never knew because of that war and the enemy they were fighting.

I was moved to tears that day. I found out what happened to L/Sergeant Oswald James Griffin of "C" Company, 5th Battalion Royal Norfolk Regiment. His story is recounted in this book. Talking to those who had served with him, boxed with him, and been drilled by him, kept his memory alive.

The friendship with my pals in FEPOW Association is something I feel honoured to have and I shall treasure it forever.

As time has gone by my collection and knowledge of Royal Norfolk Regiment militaria has grown and I stage exhibitions of my own now. I also do voluntary work at the Regimental Museum housed in the Shirehall in Norwich where I have now become a familiar face. Here I found the start of the Regimental War Records for the campaign, and with help from my friend, Kate Thaxton the curator of the museum, I found the rest of the records and some diaries kept in secret in prison camps. Using "The Britannia Magazine", August 1946, and "The Royal Norfolk Regiment 1919-1951" as a basis I was able to compile a history of each of the three Battalions up to and after the Fall of Singapore.

This brief history was put on show for the first time at an exhibition of Far Eastern War memorabilia, owned by Vic Brown and myself, staged by Dereham Antiquarian Society, helped by Dereham Branch of FEPOW, held on Saturday, 15th February, 1992, to mark the 50th Anniversary of the Fall of Singapore. Almost 600 veterans and visitors passed through the doors on that day. Seeing my accounts of the various Battalions during the war many veterans enlarged on the stories recorded there, recounting their exploits during the last days of Singapore and life in the Japanese Concentration Camps. So many of them asked for copies, it appeared that there was no readily available publication specifically recounting their experiences. Hence I have compiled this book, the story of what really happened to the 4th, 5th and 6th (Territorial) Battalions, 1939 to 1945 — "To Singapore and Beyond".

Neil Storey, 1992

The 4th Battalion

(This section is based on the account compiled by Lieut-Col. E. C. Knights, MC, MM, TD)

'A' Company, 4th Battalion, Royal Norfolk Regiment, at Duckworth Mill, Blackburn, 1941

The telegram ordering mobilisation was received on September 1st, 1939, and the under overall command of Lieut. Col. J. H. Jewson, MC, TD, and his Second-in-Command, Major A. E. Knights, MC, MM, the embodiment was carried out. In general the Companies remained at their home stations, the structure of the Battalion being as follows:

Commanding:
LIEUT. COL J. H. JEWSON, MC, TD

Second-in-Command:
MAJOR A. E. KNIGHTS, MC, MM

Adjutant:
MAJOR S. J. POPE

Quartermaster:
MAJOR W. F. CHAPMAN

Signals Officer:
LIEUT. L. A. BARRETT

Transport Officer:
MAJOR J. S. CLARKE

Intelligence Officer:
LIEUT. J. M. DRANE

HQ Company:
CAPT. R. F. HUMPHREY

'A' Company:
CAPT. A. E. TUNBRIDGE

'B' Company:
CAPT. W. L. FAUX

'C' Company:
CAPT. L. H. TIBBENHAM

'D' Company:
MAJOR F. P. MOLYNEUX

The full strength on mobilisation was 29 officers, 39 warrant officers and sergeants, and 607 other ranks, a total of 675 all ranks. On September 2nd four sergeants and 91 other ranks were transferred to the 6th Battalion, leaving a total of 551 other ranks. The Battalion was brigaded with the 4th and 5th Battalions, The Suffolk Regiment, to form 54 Infantry Brigade, under Brig. E. H. W. Backhouse, as part of 18th Infantry Division.

The early weeks of the war were spent largely in providing guards on vulnerable points and aerodromes, although as much individual training was carried out as possible under the rather difficult and scattered conditions. A move in October to Gorleston brought the Battalion together as a unit, with Battalion H.Q., 'H.Q.' Company and two other companies in the Gorleston Holiday Camp, one company at the Great Yarmouth racecourse, and the fourth company ('D') at its home station at the York Road Drill Hall, Yarmouth. This move greatly simplified training, which was now begun in earnest. A draft of N.C.O.'s and other ranks from the 2nd Battalion proved a great help in assisting the training. In addition, parties of officers and men attended the 18th Divisional School at Cromer, and there was also a steady stream of officers and other ranks to specialist courses of instruction.

The disaster in France during May, 1940, and the end of the French participation in the war brought in its train the threat of invasion. At once the 4th Battalion was called upon for a new role, that of coast defence, and vigorous steps were taken to put it into effect. Beaches were wired, minefields laid, road blocks and strong points constructed and manned. Even a tank ditch traversed the Great Yarmouth golf course and a gap was blown in Britannia Pier to prevent its use as an enemy landing stage. However, the F.O.I.C. didn't think a good job had been made of it and ordered torpedo warheads to be installed to the seaward end of the pier with an electrical firing connection so if the enemy landed they would truly be blown sky high.

The idea was undoubtedly good, but the switch for making the necessary connection was installed beside the side of the switch which operated the beach floodlights. It was always a tense moment when orders were received to test the floodlights in case the N.C.O. in charge of the post closed the wrong switch!

It must not be forgotten, however, that the first casualties of the Battalion were incurred during this period when 2 men from 'A' Company were killed whilst laying beach mines in front of the racecourse.

54th Infantry Brigade had a stretch of 25 miles of coast to defend, from Cromer to Lowestoft, the Battalion being responsible for Great Yarmouth and Gorleston. This was no easy task, for the perimeter of the Battalion's sector measured 22 miles, but with the assistance from a Pioneer Battalion, the 8th (Home Defence) Battalion, Royal Norfolk Regiment, the 11th Battalion Norfolk Regiment Home Guard and a party of ratings from HMS Watchful, 'HQ' of the Flag Officer-in-Charge, Naval Base, Great Yarmouth, it was successfully done.

During June 1940, the strength of the Battalion was brought up to 29 officers and 950 other ranks by drafts from the I.T.C., Royal Norfolk Regiment, No. 10 Holding Battalion, at Billericay, and the I.T.C., Wiltshire Regiment. They were quickly absorbed into the Battalion and soon found their feet. Also, in June, came the first air raid warnings, the precursors of some hundreds of others during the remainder of the Battalion's stay at Yarmouth and Gorleston. Several bombs were dropped in both towns, but caused no casualties in the Battalion. During August H.M. The King, George VI, visited Battalion H.Q. and inspected a detachment of 19 officers and 323 other ranks. After the inspection His Majesty visited the officer's mess.

A move to Langley Park, Loddon, was made on September 18th. Four days later the Battalion went to "Action Stations" on receipt of the code word meaning that invasion was imminent. For twelve hours the tension remained high, men wearing gas masks for much of the time, but eventually the alarm was cancelled and the Battalion once again settled down to hard training.

By the end of 1940, with the invasion scare diminishing, and the Home Defence Units sufficiently trained and equipped to take over the duties of coast defence, 18th Infantry Division was withdrawn for more active operations. 54th Infantry Brigade was concentrated in the Cambridge area for more specialised training, and for the next two and a half months all ranks were hard at work, with frequent specialist courses to bring variety to the training. Gradually the 4th Battalion was taking real shape and settling down into an efficient and well trained unit.

Shortly before Christmas 18th Division received orders to proceed overseas to Egypt, there to complete training. As a preliminary it was ordered to Scotland and on January 8th, 1941, 54th Brigade was concentrated near Hawick. The Battalion was quartered in Stobs Camp, about five miles from Hawick, together with 4th Suffolks and soon settled down to the Scottish scene. The first few weeks were intensely cold, 38° of frost being recorded on January 18th and deep snow lying on the hill-sides. This lasted until well on into February and interfered considerably with training, although it served an excellent purpose in toughening up the Battalion and in bringing opportunities for ski-ing.

During March, Brigade and Divisional schemes were carried out to exercise the movement of troops, to test marching powers, and to practise the seizing and holding of bridgehead positions with a Brigade Group. It was all very strenuous – on one occasion the Battalion marched 22 miles in one day from Hawick to Melrose – but it was excellent training and by the time the next move came along, the whole brigade was working together as a team.

The decision to move 18th Division to Egypt to finish its training there was cancelled in the early part of 1941, a change of plan that was to have far-reaching effects on the Battalion when its turn came for action. Instead of Egypt, 54th Brigade moved to Blackburn in mid-April, the division here being under the command of Major Gen. M. B. Beckwith-Smith. Divisional exercises were continued in the neighbourhood throughout May, and in June the Battalion underwent a two-day endurance test, consisting of a route march, night operations, a scheme which included field firing, and a final route march back to Blackburn. All ranks came through it well, earning the congratulations of the Divisional Commander and the Brigadier.

From Blackburn the Battalion moved on August 13th to Ross-on-Wye for the next stage of its training. This consisted at first of route marches, with a return across country in the fastest possible time, and also of night operations. Later it included river crossings in assault boats, both by day and night.

Lieut. Col. Jewson was promoted on September 9th, and was succeeded in command of the Battalion by Lieut. Col. Knights. Both had contributed greatly to the mounting efficiency, having been with the Battalion since its mobilisation at the beginning of the war. Major J. N. Packard became Second-in-Command in place of Lieut. Col. Knights.

The Battalion, with other units in the division stationed in the vicinity of Ross-on-Wye, was inspected by H.M. The King shortly before leaving the area. On this occasion Lieut. Col. Knights was decorated by the King, receiving from him the Territorial Decoration. This was a rather unique honour, as His Majesty did not usually make a personal decoration of this nature.

During September, instructions were received by the Battalion to hold itself in readiness for operations overseas. Tropical kit was issued, vehicles prepared for shipment, and reinforcements received to replace men unfit for service abroad. On October 28th most of 18th Infantry Division proceeded to Liverpool, where it embarked in a fleet of transports, the Battalion sailing in the *Andes*. The destination was unknown, but there was a tremendous feeling of excitement, and also of relief, that at last the long months of training were past and that the future held hopes of more stirring days.

The convoy, heavily escorted by destroyers, sailed out into the Atlantic on October 29th. On November 2nd, midway between Great Britain and Canada, an American squadron, including a battleship and the aircraft carrier *Lexington*, took over the escort duties and it became known that the first destination was Halifax, Nova Scotia. Here the *Andes* went alongside and the Battalion transhipped into the American transport *Wakefield*, a ship of 27,000 tons. The voyage was continued on November 10th, the convoy now consisting of six American troopships escorted by the aircraft carrier *Ranger*, two cruisers, and eight destroyers. Still the final destination of the division was unknown.

A month later the convoy steamed into Cape Town. By now the Japanese attack on Pearl Harbour had taken place and the United States was in the war. The Japanese landing in Malaya was still in its initial stages, and the fact of war in the Far East gave to some a suspicion of the final destination of the division, although the most popular guess was Suez and the Middle East.

Three days were spent in Cape Town, giving all ranks a chance to stretch their legs and enjoy the lavish hospitality of the inhabitants. On the 13th the convoy left again, steaming up the East African coast past Madagascar and then out into the Indian Ocean. It was announced on the 18th that the final destination of 18th Division was Bombay, which was reached on December 27th, after a total sea journey of 17,011 miles.

The Battalion disembarked on the 28th and moved by train with the remainder of the brigade to Ahmednagar. Here a certain amount of further training was carried out, though the heat during the day made conditions arduous. Added difficulties arose from the fact that the Battalion's transport was in another ship and had not yet arrived, and that the Battalion was held in constant readiness for a further move.

It came on January 11th, 1942, with orders to proceed to Bombay. Even though the final destination was still a secret, few could now doubt that this was the first step towards Malaya, where the Japanese had been advancing with alarming rapidity down the peninsula and where the situation was already becoming critical. At Bombay, reached on January 15th, 54th Brigade once again embarked in the U.S.S. *Wakefield,* with the remainder of the division in other ships. The convoy sailed at 1300 hours on the 19th, its destination being given as the South-West Pacific area. Pamphlets on jungle warfare were issued, and all ranks attempted to learn something of the new type of warfare which lay ahead. As the convoy passed through the Banka Straits on January 28th, it was sighted by a Japanese plane which dropped six bombs without result. That night, to avoid any bunching of the ships in narrow waters, the three fastest vessels were ordered ahead a full speed. The U.S.S. *Wakefield* won the race to Singapore and 54th Brigade disembarked in Keppel Harbour, Singapore, on the 29th. Although the news from Malaya was not encouraging, spirits were high in the Battalion. It could not yet be known that, within a period of 17 days, all the months of hard training since 1939 were to be wasted. The curtain was only just beginning to rise on the last act of the great tragedy.

The battle for Singapore fell into two distinct phases and during the first, from January 29th to February 9th, there was little activity for the Battalion. 18 Infantry Division was responsible for the defence of the North-Eastern sector of Singapore Island, their area stretching from Fairy Point, near Changi, on the right, to Seeltar Aerodrome on the left, and extending as far south as the Tampines Road and Thompson Village, near MacRitchie Reservoir. On disembarkation the Battalion was taken by lorries to a tented camp on the Tampines Road and, during their second night under canvas, the last British troops to escape from the mainland of Malaya made their way to the Island over the Causeway across Johore Straits. The Causeway was blown behind them and Singapore Island, separated from the mainland, was hurriedly prepared for a last stand against the enemy.

Already the difficulties of defence were being appreciated. Perhaps the most obvious was the complete lack of fighter cover overhead, leaving the air for the Japanese bombers, who made the most of their opportunity. There was, too, a shortage of full equipment, some not landed from the transports until February 8th, some lost in the daily air attacks on the dock areas of Singapore. A third reason was the thinness of Allied troops on the ground, for Singapore Island is roughly 20 miles long by 10 miles wide, and the defenders consisted of 18th Division, less one Brigade, 11th Indian Division, with 53rd Infantry Brigade under command, and the remains of an Australian Division. None, except for a few of the Indians and some of the Australians, had been trained in jungle warfare.

For the first few days the Battalion remained in brigade reserve to form a force for counter-attack should the Japanese attempt a landing in the brigade area. Battalion H.Q., H.Q. Company (Major R. F. Humphrey) and 'A' Company (Capt. M. Gowing) were stationed in the Teck Hock area, 'B' Company (Major W. L. Faux) about two miles from Teck Hock, 'C' Company (Capt. T. C. Eaton) in the Serangoon Jetty area, and 'D' Company (Capt. T. F. Phillips) in the Serangoon Church area. Frequent reconnaissances were carried out by officers and N.C.O.'s with the object of becoming familiar with the country over which the Battalion would have to operate, and especially with the best lines of approach in the forward area.

The only brush with the enemy during these days occurred during the night of February 7th–8th, when the Japanese attacked the Island of Ubin, which lay in the Straits on the right of the brigade sector and was occupied as an outpost by alternate platoons of 'C' and 'D' Companys. The enemy attack coincided with the normal relief of the occupying platoon, and the relieving platoon had just reached the landing beach as the others retire on to it.

The enemy was estimated at about 1,000, and four men were cut off during the withdrawal to the beach. On the following night a patrol under Lieut. P. C. Barr returned to the island but found it deserted and with no traces of the four men who had failed to return.

The night marked the end of the first phase in the defence of Singapore Island. The second began with the forcing by the enemy of the Straits of Johore, where they narrowed to a width of about half a mile in the west. That night they penetrated the forward defences, manned by the Australians, and by the morning of the 9th had advanced to a depth of about two miles. Here they began fanning out into a three-pronged attack, the northern aimed at Pierce Reservoir and Seletar Aerodrome, the centre at the MacRitchie Reservoir, and the southern one at the village of Bukit Timah.

On the morning of February 10th the Battalion received orders to form part of a composite force under the command of Lieut. Col. L. C. Thomas, Royal Northumberland Fusiliers. It was called 'Tomforce' and its object was to back-up 12th (Indian) Brigade and to stem the tide of the enemy advance towards Bukit Timah. At 1230 hours the force proceeded in buses to the Bukit Timah Road, advancing on the northern side of it towards the village. On the south side of the road a similar advance was made by the 1/5th Sherwood Foresters.

That night the Japanese captured the village. On the morning of the 11th the Battalion continued the advance through the thickly wooded country on a two-company front, 'A' followed by 'D' Company on the left, 'B' followed by 'C' on the right. There was considerable enemy activity in the air and as 'B' Company reached its first objective it was subjected to a low-level bombing attack. Its position, too, was marked by smoke signals dropped by the attacking aircraft, followed by heavy machine-gun and mortar fire from concealed Japanese positions. 'B' and 'C' Companys both suffered heavy casualties, but continued the advance after the carrier platoon had given some support with 2-in. mortars. Once again it ran into heavy opposition, with a withering fire from the enemy on high ground to the north. It was obvious from this attack that the Japanese were infiltrating straight to the northward of the 'Tomforce' position, and that their objective was the reservoir near Thompson Village. After consultation with the Force Commander, it was decided to withdraw the Battalion to the area of Singapore Racecourse in an effort to beat back this advance. As good a position as possible was selected and occupied on the racecourse, and contact made with the 4th Suffolks on the right to form a perimeter defence covering the MacRitchie Reservoir.

A blunder on the night of the 11th made the situation worse. The 4th Suffolks were ordered to advance towards the Swiss Rifle Club Hill, near the junction of the Bukit Timah road, an objective impossible to reach because of the Japanese strength on the high ground to the north. All it did was to uncover the right flank of the Battalion, a situation of which the enemy took full advantage. By first light on the 12th the Battalion was almost completely surrounded, with only one small gap left to the eastward.

At 0900 hours on the 12th the Japanese put in a heavy attack on the forward company, 'A', which was astride the Bukit Timah road. The enemy used tanks in this attack, which caused several casualties, and forced the company to withdraw. The C.O. at once planned a counter-attack to restore the position, but before it could be mounted, orders were received to withdraw the whole Battalion to Adam Road, running south from the MacRitchie Reservoir. The withdrawal was carried out successfully through the open gap to the eastward of the Battalion positions, with the exception of the carriers, which had to run the gauntlet of the Bukit Timah road. Here they came up against enemy tanks, but successfully fought their way past without loss, a wonderful achievement of the crews who, at one time, had seemed to be facing almost certain annihilation.

Back again at Adam Road, the Battalion once again came under the command of 54th Infantry Brigade, 'Tomforce' being dissolved. The positions were put into as strong a state of defence as possible, barbed wire being used as an added deterrent against attacks. A reasonably quiet night on February 12th–13th, although it gave some opportunity to the tired troops of catching up on their sleep, proved only the prelude of a heavy attack on the 13th, enemy shelling and mortaring causing further casualties in the Battalion. The attack itself was largely broken up by fire from supporting artillery, although in the afternoon a further heavy shelling added to the casualties. During the evening of the 13th the Battalion was relieved on the western side of Adam Road by the 1/5 Sherwood Foresters, withdrawing into brigade reserve on the east side of the road.

Shelling continued through the night of February 13th–14th, allowing only little sleep, and proving also that the enemy was well informed of the Battalion position. The firing became heavier during the morning of the 14th, added to by repeated bombing attacks, and again there were many casualties. The enemy put in several determined attacks, one breaking through to the north of the Battalion positions and a second, made in the early hours of the 15th, forcing back the Sherwood Foresters. 'B' and 'C' Companys were ordered to counter attack and, by 1100 hours, had restored the position, although at a very heavy cost in casualties.

In the meantime, the situation in the rest of the Island had become critical. The speed of the enemy advance had been so rapid that 11th (Indian) Division had been overrun, and the Commander-in-Chief had been forced to abandon the defence of the northern beaches. Singapore itself was in a sorry state, its streets choked with rubble from repeated bombing attacks, and the harbour area in a state of chaos as attempts were made to evacuate civilian and non-combatant personnel. As rumour succeeded rumour, it became obvious to all that the end could not be far off.

It came with dramatic suddenness. At about noon on the 15th a car was seen proceeding along the Bukit Timah road flying a white flag above a Union Jack. Even though it was at first thought to be a Japanese fifth-column trick, it had a depressing effect on morale. An hour or so later news was received from Brigade H.Q. that firing would cease at 1600 hours. Although this was later altered to 2000 hours, it made little difference to the feeling of bitter disappointment among all ranks. The end had indeed come, and the future held only dim and doubtful visions of the unknown horrors of prison camp.

DOMAIN OF NEPTUNUS REX

TO ALL SAILORS WHEREVER YE MAY BE, and to all Mermaids, Sea Serpents, Whales, Sharks, Porpoises, Dolphins, Skates, Eels, Suckers, Lobsters, Crabs, Pollywogs, and other Living Things of the Sea:

Greeting: KNOW YE, That on this 24th. day of November, 1941 in Latitude 00000 and Longitude 47 there appeared within the limit of our Royal Domain the U.S.S. WAKEFIELD, bound Southward for the Equator and South Africa. BE IT REMEMBERED, That the said vessel and its Officers and Crew thereof, have been inspected and passed on by Ourself and Our Royal Staff. AND BE IT KNOWN, By all Sailors, Marines, Landlubbers and others who may be honored by his presence, that Pte.Osborne R. of the Royal Norfolk Regt.

having been found worthy to be numbered as ONE OF OUR TRUSTY SHELLBACKS, has been gathered to our fold and duly initiated into the Solemn Mysteries of the

ANCIENT ORDER OF THE DEEP

BE IT FURTHER UNDERSTOOD, That by virtue of power invested in me, I do hereby command all my subjects to show due honor and respect to him wherever he may enter into Our Realm.

DISOBEY THIS ORDER UNDER PENALTY OF OUR ROYAL DISPLEASURE

Given Under Our Hand and Seal this 24th. day of November, 1941

DAVEY JONES
His Majesty's Scribe

W. K. SCAMMELL, Comdr.,
U.S. Coast Guard,
Commanding, U.S.S.WAKEFIELD.

NEPTUNUS REX
Ruler of the Raging Main

Certificate individually presented to men of the 4th Battalion who 'Crossed the Line' aboard USS Wakefield

The 5th Battalion

(This section is based on the account written by Major Crane)

Members of the 5th Battalion guarding His Majesty King George VI at Sandringham, December 1939

When the Territorial Army was embodied on the outbreak of war, the 5th Battalion were in rather a peculiar position. Earlier in the year, the Territorial Army was doubled, the result of this was that practically up to the time of going to camp in August, 1939, recruits were joining. It was therefore decided not to form two Battalions until 1st October thus allowing the new unit to grow up alongside the trained one. The Battalion area would be separated geographically so that each Battalion would be approximately the same strength.

When embodiment was ordered the 7th Battalion immediately moved its H.Q. to King's Lynn. The 5th Battalion embodied at the following places:— Dereham, Aylsham, North Walsham, and Holt. The troops were billeted with subsistence in the towns. Later, messing was carried out centrally in each station. A large detachment was sent to form part of the I.T.C. at Norwich, and Officers and N.C.O.'s attended a Brigade cadre course at Norwich. These latter formed the staff of the Battalion cadres held in Dereham. At the same time guards were found for various aerodromes and vulnerable points in the area.

During early October, the invasion scare started, and the Battalion was concentrated at Holt at very short notice (about 24 hours). Again the troops were billeted and dining halls requisitioned. Shortly afterwards the Battalion was moved to Weybourne A.A. practice camp and accommodated in huts. It was designed only as a summer camp and offered very little protection from the 1939/40 winter, even the sea froze during one of the coldest winters known. During this time Cadres, Individual and Section training was carried out, also troops were still manning vulnerable points. Positions were sited for the defence of a large area of the coast. Another army class joined and were trained here. At the same time a large number of men who were under 19 were transferred to the A.A. Command. In December, Capt. J. Alley took over Adjutant from Major H. T. Crane who had been Adjutant since 1936. At Christmas, the Battalion had the honour of providing a guard for His Majesty the King during his stay for about six weeks at Sandringham. The guard was about a company strong under:—Major E. Thistleton-Smith, Capt. E. P. Hansell, Capt. T. D. Savory, Lt J. M. Woodhouse (The Essex Regiment attached).

12

It was quartered in York Cottage. Its duties consisted of manning L.M.G., A.A. posts and patrolling the grounds.

In March, 1940, Lt.-Col. E. C. Prattley came from the 2nd Battalion in France to take over command from Lt.-Col. G. N Scott-Chad. After Dunkirk, the Battalion occupied their Beach Defence positions almost continually. Defences and anti-tank ditches were dug and wired and a field of fire cleared. At the same time, when possible; training was carried out. Later in the summer as vehicles and carriers arrived, more advanced training was undertaken. In September, the Battalion went into Brigade reserve and was billeted in Holt. The bulk of the Battalion were in Gresham School. Brigade and Battalion training was carried out with a fairly complete establishment of vehicles. Major E. Thistleton-Smith went to command the Young Soldiers Battalion and Major Crane returned from working on the G.H.Q. Defence Line and was appointed Second in Command

In November the Battalion was moved to King's Lynn and were billeted in the warehouses on the Docks - these were cold, dark, and uncomfortable. Whilst here a few bombs were dropped by German aircraft. In December, Capt. M. T. Keith took over Adjutant as Capt. Alley was invalided out of the service.

The Battalion were again chosen to provide a guard during His Majesty's stay at Sandringham, but owing to the impending move and mobilisation, the guard had to be relieved and one provided by another unit.

In January, 1941, the 18th Division was ordered to mobilise in South Scotland. The troops went by train; transport by road, staying en route at Doncaster, Catterick and Carlisle. Battalion H.Q. and 3 Companys went to Castle Douglas, 2 Company went to Dalbeattie. Everyone was accommodated in billets. The local people were most hospitable. Intense training was carried out including Divisional Schemes - the Battalion was now becoming very fit and well trained and most of the mobilisation equipment had arrived.

Except for the raid on Glasgow, this area was 'siren free' which was a great relief after the East Coast.

In March much to everyone's surprise the Division was ordered to move to the West of England, the 53rd Brigade to occupy an area in Cheshire. The bulk of the Brigade went by road staying at Preston in the Depot of the East Lancashire Regiment and the Loyal Regiment. This journey of 186 miles was long and tiring owing to the number of towns which had to be passed through. The Battalion was accommodated at Marbury Hall, Northwich, mostly in huts which were quite comfortable. Considerable training was carried out here and a good deal of participation in Home Guard exercises and training.

In September, orders were received to prepare to go overseas. On the 25th October, the Battalion sent an advance party to the ship. This included O.C. Ship, Ship's Adjutant, R.S.M. and O.R. Clerk. On 28th October, the Battalion embarked on the S.S. Duchess of Atholl, in peace time a C.P.R. Liner of about 21,000 tons. The following Officers and N.C.O.'s embarked with the Battalion:-

Commanding:
Lieut. Col. E. C. Prattley

2nd in Command:
Major H. T. Crane

Adjutant:
Capt. M. T. Keith

Quartermaster:
Lieut. G. Clarke

Carrier Officer:
Capt. B. Savory

Signal Officer:
Capt. D. R. Gray

Int. Officer:
Lieut. K. A. S. Potter

Defence Pl.:
Lieut. C. J. Brereton

A.A.:
Lieut. T. W. Higgs

M.T.O.:
Lieut. L. A. Collins

Mortars:
Lieut. W. B. Battersby

Pioneers:
Lieut. P. G. Bambridge

Interpreters:
Capt. F. Wallace and
Lieut. R. Carey, f.m.s.v.f.
joined on arrival in Singapore

Medical Officer:
CAPT. R. W. W. BROWN, R.A.M.C.

R.S.M.:
R.S.M. BURROWS, L.G.

'A' Company:
CAPT. R. HAMOND
CAPT. H. E. SCHULMAN
LIEUT. LEE-SMITH
LIEUT. P. J. RAMM
LIEUT. TURNER
C.S.M. W. A. STEPHENSON

'B' Company:
CAPT. A. J. SELF
CAPT. R. A. FERRIER
LIEUT. G. H. PALLISTER
LIEUT. MCKEAN
LIEUT. P. J. SAYER
C.S.M. T. BRANDWOOD

'C' Company:
MAJOR C. P. WOOD
LIEUT. T. R. CUBITT
LIEUT. J. TAYLOR
LIEUT. F. W. W. KETTLEY
LIEUT. W. J. WARRINGTON
C.S.M. W. MELTON

'D' Company:
CAPT. S. C. H. BOARDMAN
LIEUT. R. A. BOWMAN
LIEUT. H. R. COOK
LIEUT. R. A. BURNE
C.S.M. A. E. PATRICK

H.Q. Company:
CAPT. E. P. HANSELL

First Reinforcements:
MAJOR R. C. BRIEGEL
LIEUT. J. V. WILLINS
LIEUT. E. F. ADIE
LIEUT. L. W. CURTIS
LIEUT. E. A. PARKER
C.S.M. H. WARD

Chaplain.:
REV. J. O. DEAN, C.F.

Posted to H.Q. 53rd Brigade:
CAPT. C. S. M. BRERETON

Posted to 198 Field. Amb.:
CAPT. J. HENDRY, R.A.M.C.

The ship left the Clyde the next day and met other ships from the West Coast ports, carrying the Division. There was a small escort of a couple of destroyers. About halfway across the Atlantic, a very big convoy was sighted which seemed to stretch right across the horizon. Presently the air was alive with planes flying round the ships which, much to everyone's surprise, turned out to be U.S.A. planes. Our escort was now relieved by U.S.A. ships consisting of a battleship, a large aircraft carrier, two 10,000 ton cruisers, and about six destroyers. Needless to say, everyone felt rather more secure.

The weather was very kind for the time of year and later became quite calm. There was about 2,500 troops on board the ship which was more comfortable than the peacetime troopers and very good food was served. After an uneventful voyage of about eight days the convoy entered Halifax. Here the Division transhipped into U.S.A. ships. The Battalion embarked on the '*Mount Vernon,*' formally the U.S. Liner '*Washington*' of about 26,000 tons. The troops were rather crowded but quite comfortable having iron and canvas berths to sleep upon. After a stay of about 24 hours, the Division left Halifax with a big escort.

A few days later the weather became much warmer and battle dress was discarded for khaki drill. The first stop was Trinidad. No-one was allowed ashore here but it looked a very beautiful island. After taking on water and fuel the voyage continued in calm warm weather. The 'crossing the line' ceremony was held on 23rd November in about long. 40 degrees 41' W. just off the South American coast. Training and games were held on deck during the day and concerts in the evenings. The one drawback was that in accordance with United States Navy Orders, the ship was 'dry.' Before making Cape Town, the convoy went far South down into the 'Roaring Forties' or 'Westerlies,' but a ship of that size was fairly steady in the following wind, although the escorting cruisers and destroyers had rather a rough time.

The convoy arrived at Cape Town in mid December. Everyone was given a very good time by the local residents, who set themselves out to give all ranks as much entertainment as possible; in fact the South African Ports had a high reputation for the way in which they entertained convoys passing through. Everyone was sorry to leave.

Soon after sailing it was disclosed that our destination should have been the Middle East but that it had been altered to Singapore. T.E.W.T.S. and lectures on Malaya now became the universal form of training. The convoy proceed up the African coast and went between the mainland and Madagascar. The *'Mount Vernon'* then received orders to proceed at once to Mombassa. The ship left the convoy and went towards the African coast at about 21 knots. Mombassa was reached on Christmas Day. All ranks were given shore leave and bathing parties were organised. After a couple of days the ship sailed and joined a convoy bound for the Far East.

The next call was a fuelling station in the Indian ocean and after a short stay of about 6 hours, the convoy put to sea again. The convoy passed through the Sunda Strait between Sumatra and Java and sailed up the Banka Strait to Singapore During this latter part of the voyage there were heavy tropical rain storms which probably prevented the convoy being sighted by enemy aircraft. The ship went into the large graving dock in the Naval base and the troops disembarked in pouring rain on Friday, 13th January, 1942.

The Battalion was quartered in the Woodlands Camp near the Naval base; this was a comfortable hutted camp. The next two days was spent in getting ready to go into battle. The Battalion transport had not arrived, so new transport had to be drawn and organised on a different scale. In the evening, all officers were given a lecture by Lt.-General Percival on the campaign, and lectures on Japanese tactics were given to all ranks by Officers and other ranks who had already had battle experience in Malaya. On the 16th January, the Commanding Officer with a Reconnaissance party reported to the 2/M. Battalion, A.I.F. at Jemalung on the East Coast of Johore. The next day the Battalion moved by M.T. to Ayer Hitam in the centre of Johore. The first reinforcements were left in Singapore.

As the Battalion was about to take up a defensive position that evening in the village of Yongpeng, orders were received to move to Jemaluang next morning. On the 18th, the Battalion moved to Jemaluang by M.T. and took up the prepared defensive position from the A.I.F. which had previously been reconnoitred. The next day patrols were sent out and at noon orders were received to move back to Ayer Hitam. Owing to shortage of transport this had to be done in two relays. The 20th was spent in a harbouring area, the Battalion being in 11th Indian Division Reserve.

On the 21st, patrols were sent out and contacted the enemy, two men being wounded and one missing. During the evening the road to Batu-Pahat on the west coast was reported blocked. At dawn on the 22nd, patrols made contact with the troops from Batu Pahat at the 73rd mile stone and reported the road open. The Battalion was ordered to keep the road open throughout the day. At about 1600 hours, 'D' Company made contact with the enemy near the 73rd mile stone. One platoon was ambushed and Capt. Boardman was killed, Capt. Schulman taking over. Orders for the Battalion to move into Batu Pahat were received about 1730 hours. In the meantime, it was reported that the road was again blocked. The Battalion was then ordered to concentrate for the night near the 72nd mile stone and move on Batu Pahat next morning. On the morning of the 23rd, at dawn the advance guard encountered a strongly defended road block. 'B' Company attacked the block but was unsuccessful, suffering several casualties including Sec. Lieut. McKean killed and Lieut. Pallister seriously wounded (later died of wounds). 'C' Company attacked round the South flank and got two platoons round the block but had not again reached the road, when at 11.30 the Division Commander ordered the Battalion to withdraw back to Ayer Hitam.

At 1300 hours, orders were received to move to Batu Pahat by M.T. taking the road South and then up the West coast via Skudai and Pontain Kechil. The Battalion moved at 1600 hours and harboured for the night near Skudai. On the 24th January, the Battalion left the harbouring area at 0400 hours and arrived two miles south of Batu Pahat at 0700 hours where contact was made with H.Q. 15th Brigade. The 2nd Cambridgeshire Regiment had been ordered to withdraw from the town the previous evening but had been stopped when just clear of the town. The Battalion was ordered to retake positions in the centre and East of the town. The attack commenced at 1045 hours assisted by one troop R.A. which could only shoot by the map. This attack was successful on the left but the right sector became heavily engaged. No further forward movement was possible owing to the difficulty of getting support of 3" mortars and R.A. In addition there were indications of a threat from two high points east of the main road. At 1500 hours, 'B' Company

15

was ordered to occupy these features which it did. It was attacked and had to withdraw below the crest. It was then decided to regain these positions at night.

At 0400 hours on the 25th January, 'C' Company, with the remainder of one Company and Cambridgeshire Regiment attacked; this was unsuccessful although a position was reached just short of the crest. Heavy mortar and L.M.G. fire was experienced. At about 13.00 hours the Battalion was ordered to hold its present position and cover the withdrawal of 2nd Cambridgeshire Regiment and then withdraw. The positions were finally abandoned at about 2100 hours. The Battalion marched back about four miles and were ferried by M.T. to a position near the aerodrome arriving at midnight. On the morning of 26th, information was received that the road in rear of the Battalion position had been blocked by the enemy in several places. At approximately 1000 hours, the Battalion was ordered to move South, sending all transport ahead. At this time some 250 vehicles were on the road, head to tail, waiting to get back when the blocks had been cleared. At 1745 hours, the Brigade Commander ordered all transport to be destroyed and all men to make their way south through the jungle and collect about 18 miles back. A bridge across the river was to be blown at 1830 hours. At this time all ranks were extremely tired having had very little sleep since they landed.

On the 27th January, the majority of the Battalion, about 500, under Major Wood and guided by Capt. F. Wallace reached Bennut and were taken back by M.T. to B echelon, near Skudai. Another party under Capt. Schulman made for the coast and were taken off by the Navy. The Commanding Officer blew up the bridge, got separated from the Battalion but eventually, with about eight men, the party made their way down the coast in a small canoe.

On the 28th, the main party was taken into Serangoon Road Camp in Singapore by M.T. From the 29th January to 2nd February, the Battalion reorganised, re-equipped and rested. The first reinforcement also joined the Battalion. On the 3rd February, the Battalion proceeded to the Naval Base on the North of the Island and began to put in into a state of defence. During this time all forces were leaving the mainland and coming back to defend the island. On the 4th February, the Battalion worked on the defences, digging, wiring and sandbagging. Shelling commenced and Battalion Headquarters had to move twice. This shelling continued on the 5th, 6th and 7th February, the Battalion suffering some casualties including Major Wood wounded. Major Crane left to take command of the 6th Battalion.

On the 7th February, Lieut. Potter and Lieut. R. Carey (F.M.S.V.F.) and three other ranks went across the Strait of Johore and spent 24 hours on enemy territory. Work continued on the defences and on the 9th, 10th and 11th, R.E. demolition parties began blowing up the dockyard.

On the 12th February, the Battalion was ordered to withdraw finally taking over an area on the perimeter of Singapore City. 'D' Company, who always seemed to be the rear-guard, was the last official company out of the Naval Base, everything was being looted and was under heavy fire. This was necessary owing to a successful enemy landing on the west coast of the Island. During the withdrawal, the Battalion suffered several casualties from air attacks. On the 13th, the Battalion took up a defensive position in the Braddell Road area. During the early part of the night, the right forward platoon of 'A' Company was attacked. This attack was beaten off with few casualties. Heavy firing and shelling continued all night. It was from the fighting, much of which was literally hand to hand in this area, that the Battalion sustained heavy casualties.

In the early hours of Saturday 14th, many men from the Battalion were evacuated to Alexandra Military Hospital. The water supply to the Hospital had been cut off in the early hours, and shelling from the air, mortar and artillery, became intense. Having penetrated from the Ayer Rajah area the first Japanese attacks were seen towards the Sister' Quarters, the Japanese fighting troops were about to enter the hospital from the rear. Lieut. E. Weston went from the Recreation Room to the rear entrance with a white flag to indicate surrender of the hospital. The Japanese took no notice and bayoneted him to death. They then entered the ground floor of the Hospital and ran amok and neither incumbents pointing to the Red Cross brassards or shouting the word 'Hospital!' had any effect.

Next a Japanese party entered the Theatre Block where operations were being prepared. In the corridors male and female personnel held up their hands but the Japs, for no reason, set among them, flailing bayonets. Even a soldier on the operating table was bayoneted to death.

Realising the situation Sergeant Oswald Griffin, of 'C' Company, although wounded himself, mustered those he could to hold back the attackers and assist those who could escape to British lines. Sergeant Griffin and his small group of brave men were never seen again.

Early on the 14th a heavy attack on the 2nd Cambridgeshire Regiment area resulted in the Battalion left flank being exposed. The line was readjusted by a counter attack by 2nd Cambridgeshire Regiment. During the night, the enemy infiltrated on the left flank and established several posts in 'C' Company Reserve platoon area. The R.A. support was excellent when S.O.S. fire was called for by 'C' Company. It is traditional that the British Army never lets a complete unit be taken prisoners of war consequently, on the 13th, the official escape party consisting of three officers and about eight other ranks were ordered away. They were lucky and all, except one who was recaptured, eventually reached India via Java

On the 15th, the enemy attacked on the Battalion front from dawn until 1600 hours, when the order came through to cease fire as the garrison had been ordered to capitulate. That night was the first sleep many had had for some time The strength of the Battalion on the capitulation was 30 officers and 660 other ranks. Many others turned up later in captivity.

DECREE

Though the Empire of Nippon has been striving to settle down the Chinese incident for the sake of the East-Asian New Order and the peace of the world, England and America, helping directly and indirectly the traitor of the East-Asia, Chang Kai-Shek and disturbing the East-Asian peace without any repentance, have dared to challenge Nippon.

So, the Empire of Nippon, to give them a final blow and to rescue the East-Asian nations from the persecution of these countries, has begun to fight with them.

Look! Thais and Malayans! The East-Asian New Order is drawing quite near!

You must understand the sincere intention of Nippon, do calmly your business and co-operate with Our Army. If you disturb the works of the Nippon Army, destroying the roads, bridges and railways or acting a spy for the enemies, you will be without reserve, severely punished; on the contrary, if you co-operate with us, we will patronize you, protect your lives and fortunes and give you a reward. Look! The glorious victory is shining on the way of the Nippon Army who brings peace and happiness. You have to make an echo to the shout of triumph of Our Army and to praise the prosperity and glory of the New East-Asia.

The Commander of the Nippon Army

Leaflet of false promises and lies dropped from Japanese aircraft aimed at undermining native morale and to sabotage Allied actions in the Far East

The 6th Battalion

(This section is based on the account compiled by Lieut-Col. H. S. Ling, MC)

'A' Company, 6th Battalion, at Summer Camp, 1939

On the outbreak of war, the unit, then known as The City of Norwich Battalion, was mobilised under the command of Lieut. Col. D. G. Buxton at the Aylsham Road Drill Hall, Norwich. The Battalion was then at a very weak strength and consisted principally of recruits who had joined the Territorial Army only a few months previously.

The officers holding executive positions were:

Commanding Officer:
LIEUT. COL. D. G. BUXTON

Second-in-Command:
MAJOR H. S. LING, MC

Adjutant:
CAPT. P. M. WESTGATE

Quartermaster:
LIEUT. H. G. CLARK

'A' Company:
CAPT. H. A. COOPER

'B' Company:
LIEUT. B. O. L. PRIOR

'C' Company:
2ND LIEUT. J. FRANCIS

HQ Company:
LIEUT. R. D. T. MCCLINTOCK

'D' Company was not formed until early in 1940

Immediately after mobilisation 'A' and 'B' Companys were dispatched to Hemsby, where they were billeted in the Holiday Camp adjoining the village. 'C' Company took over guard duties at Watton Aerodrome, and the remainder of the unit remained in billets in Norwich with H.Q. at the Aylsham Road Drill Hall.

The Battalion being so weak in strength, the transfer of 16 of its best N.C.O.s to the depot at Britannia Barracks as instructors, created some difficulties in the training of the young soldiers. These troubles were, however, soon overcome by the promotion of keen and promising men, so that when the first army class draft arrived on October 19th, it was found possible to 'squad' the whole 100 recruits and commence their training without delay.

Towards the middle of November, the Battalion was ordered to Aylsham and were quartered in billets in the town, 'A' and 'B' Companys rejoining the unit from Hemsby. Here training was carried on in Blickling park, which was found a most useful area.

During the month, Major R. T. H. Reynolds, MC, joined the Battalion and was posted as O.C. 'H.Q.' Company.

After a fortnight in Aylsham a quick move was made to Sheringham, the 287 Field Company R.E. arriving in the town at the same time. All ranks were quartered in various hotels and private houses in the town, and really serious training commenced.

Shortly after arrival, the 1st Army Class, having completed their six weeks' recruit training in Norwich, rejoined the unit.

The first sight of war was seen when a German aeroplane crashed on the beach in front of the Grand Hotel, and its occupants all killed or drowned. The R.A.F. arrived quickly and parts of the aeroplane was taken away by them for closer inspection, but not before some unauthorised trophies were secured by those of the Battalion near at hand which were handed over later.

The first war Christmas was celebrated here and the whole Battalion sat down in the basement of the Grand Hotel to an excellent dinner of turkey and plum pudding. The C.O., Lieut. Col. D. G. Buxton, visited each company in turn, and 'took wine' with each mess room. He was entertained afterwards in the Sergeants' Mess.

On the evening of Christmas Day, when 25 per cent of the unit were on leave, a 'stand-to' was ordered, and positions on the coast were manned for several hours.

January 1940 was a cold and bitter month with heavy snowfalls and parties were sent out frequently to clear the roads of snowdrifts to make way for the passage of the Battalion Transport (which then consisted of impressed civilian vehicles) to get through to Dereham to collect the rations. After the snow had partially disappeared the roads were so icy that it was found quite impractical to carry out the normal route marches which were usually held at least once a week.

With the return of the Army Class it was now found possible to form 'D' Company under the command of Major R. Graham, IARO, who had recently joined the Battalion.

As the weather improved, considerable use was made of the golf course for training, and the hills and rough ground to the south of the town and towards Cromer, and, in spite of the location of two rifle companies at various aerodromes in North Norfolk, considerable progress was made in the efficiency of the Battalion as a fighting unit. Drill was also not forgotten, and Battalion parades on a Saturday morning were the usual feature.

During the spring, Capt. J. M. Smyth joined from the Jersey Militia, where he had been serving as Adjutant, and Major H. S. Ling, MC, and Major R. T. H. Reynolds, MC, changed appointments at their mutual request.

The military position now being serious, the Battalion took up defensive positions along the coast from Cromer on the right to Weybourne on the left, and a Lewis gun post located at East Runton claimed a German aeroplane which was brought down to the east of Cromer.

At the end of May, Lieut. Col. F. L. Cubitt relieved Lieut. Col. D. G. Buxton in command, and, the military position being even worse, the whole Battalion remained in the defensive positions they had dug, sleeping and eating in their battle positions and working during all the hours of daylight on improvements to their trenches. Everyone 'stood-to' for an hour before dusk and until well after dark, and again at an hour before dawn.

In June, large drafts from the Northamptonshire Regiment and Essex Regiment joined the Battalion, the 140 reinforcements then arriving, bringing the Battalion to somewhere near its war strength.

During July, Major R. Graham left the Battalion and was succeeded in the command of 'D' Company by Capt. J. Francis. Major R. T. H. Reynolds, MC, also left on posting to the Depot at Norwich, and Major F. M. E. D. Drake-Briscoe, arriving from the 1st Battalion, took over the duties of 2nd i/c, Capt. H. S. Cooper left to fill the vacancy in the 1st Battalion caused by the transfer of Major Briscoe, and Lieut. Col. J. F. Ross, Irish Guards, relieved Lieut. Col. F. L. Cubitt in command of the Battalion.

At the end of August, the Battalion was relieved by the 2nd Battalion the Cambridgeshire Regiment, and moved into Brigade Reserve at Holt, being quartered principally in the grounds and buildings of Gresham's School. Here there was no obstacle to training, and with the assistance of a platoon of the Irish Guards, who were attached to the Battalion for some time, Great strides were made in drill and soldierly bearing which had been somewhat forcibly necessarily neglected during the strenuous days on the coast.

During September Capt. B. O. L. Prior was posted away for duty in the Middle East, and was succeeded in command of 'B' Company by Capt. J. M. Smyth, on his return from the Senior Officers' School.

Owing to the many changes in officers there had been a number of alterations in the command of companies, and the position now was:

Commanding Officer:
Lieut. Col. J. F. Ross

Second-in-Command:
Major F. M. E. D. Drake-Briscoe

Adjutant:
Capt. P. M. Westgate

Quartermaster:
Lieut. H. G. Clarke

'H.Q.' Company:
Major S. Lyng, MC

'A' Company:
Capt. P. S. Campbell-Orde

'B' Company:
Capt. J. M. Smyth

'C' Company:
Capt. H. P. Pilkington

'D' Company:
Capt. J. Francis

In October the Battalion moved to Weybourne and took over the coastal defences from the 5th Battalion who moved into reserve in their turn. The ensuing month was spent by companies in their defensive positions, and much work was carried out in making improvements to the trenches.

In November the whole brigade moved back into reserve and the Battalion was stationed in Swaffham, where the second war Christmas was spent. The Rifle Companies were billeted in the town, and Battalion 'H.Q.' with 'H.Q.' Company at 'Petygards,' a large farm about three miles distant.

Owing to the generosity of the local townspeople, a Christmas dinner equal to that of 1939 was provided, and the C.O., Lieut. Col. J. F. Ross, visited each company in turn, and afterwards entertained all the officers at Battalion H.Q. at 'Petygards'. During this time some very good boxing shows were held in the local Territorial Drill Hall, the enthusiasm of the boxers themselves atoning fully for in some cases their lack of skill.

Early in January 1941, Major Drake-Bristoe left the unit to take command of the 1st Battalion, and so did not accompany the Battalion when it moved to Scotland on January 5th, preparatory, it was thought, to proceeding overseas. During the loading up of the Battalion stores on to the train, a German aeroplane appeared suddenly out of the low clouds and succeeded in dropping several bombs in the station yard. Unfortunately, five men were killed and one wounded as a result of this incident. Owing to the low visibility, the teams of Bren gunners stationed in the station yard did not see the plane until it was over them, and it was out of sight before effective fire could be brought to bear.

After a long night journey by train, the Battalion arrived in Dumfries and were quartered in a large mill on the outskirts of the town. The 2nd Battalion Cambridgeshire Regiment, and the Norwegian Army who were then in training in the district, comprised the remainder of the garrison of the town.

Dumfries proved to be a very happy station, and, although training was rigorous, and there were long marches into the hills, there was no sign of strain or over training. Much practice was gained in motorised movement over long distances, and the unit took part in several exercises with the remainder of the Division and other Divisions over the whole area from Dumfries to Berwick and Edinburgh.

Towards the end of March, Major A. B. Cubitt was posted to the Battalion, and took over the duties of second-in-command.

The long-expected move overseas was still postponed, although the Battalion was now fully mobilised and in possession of tropical kit, and when orders were received for a move south again it was thought for a time that the only service that would be seen would be inactive in England.

On arrival in Western Command, the Battalion was stationed in the Northwich district, the Rifle Companies being billeted in large houses and scattered over an area of about five miles with Battalion H.Q. and 'H.Q.' Company situated centrally at Sandiway.

Capt. J. Francis was now posted to another unit and Capt. P. M. Westgate, who was succeeded as Adjutant by Capt. P. R. Hill, took over the command of 'D' Company.

Many long-distance exercises were again carried out, and Shrewsbury and Birmingham were among the districts where operations took place. It was whilst the Battalion were stationed here that the first opportunity occurred of having properly organised games, and cricket matches were played against teams in the district. Efforts were made also to produce vegetables for consumption, and so relieve to some extent the increasing food shortage. Each company dug large gardens around their billets, being supplied with seeds and the proper tools by the military authorities.

In May, the enemy bombers could be heard passing overhead in their attack on Liverpool, and the Battalion was sent, two companies at a time, to take over fire-watching from the exhausted civil A.R.P. personnel. In spite of several heavy raids during the time this duty was performed, the Battalion was lucky to escape without casualties.

At the end of May, Lieut. Col. I. G. G. Lywood, who was to take the Battalion abroad, relieved Lieut. Col. J. F. Ross in command.

In the early part of June, a visit was received from the Depot Band under Bandmaster Burgess, and was much appreciated by all ranks of the Battalion. This was the first and only occasion during the war that the men of the Battalion had the privilege of hearing a military band.

In August a move was made to Knowsley Park, Lord Derby's seat, near Liverpool, where the 5th Battalion Suffolk Regiment were relieved. There were many large scale exercises during the time the Battalion was stationed in this district, and rapid moves were made to Carlisle, and the Westmorland and Yorkshire moors, including an exercise in Yorkshire with a Battalion of the then new Churchill tanks.

The weather now became much colder, and there was a great deal of heavy rain. The normal pasture of the park was churned into heavy mud, whilst the tents in which the Battalion were accommodated were invariably streaming with water. Things were so uncomfortable that a section of the 287 Field Company R.E., who arrived to erect hutments, were given a very warm welcome, and parties of men from the Battalion worked with a will under the sappers' direction to complete as soon as possible the hutted camp.

It was in October that representatives from each company were, with parties from the other two Battalions of the Brigade, reviewed by H.M. The King in Crewe Park. The troops lined each side of the drive to Crewe Hall, and the King passed down the whole lane on foot, stopping frequently and saying a few words to individual officers and men. His Majesty was greeted with hearty cheers as he approached each unit.

It was now realised that it could not be long before the Battalion realised its ambition to see active service, and everyone was 'fighting fit' when orders came for a move abroad. Some, of course, had to be left behind with the home details, but it was not known until the last moment who these unfortunates were to be. When the time came, it was found that Capt. W. G. Clarke, who had only recently joined the unit from other duties, had been selected for this duty, and, with the whole camp completely hutted, the Battalion moved to the railway station on 27th October, 1941, leaving Capt. Clarke, other officers and men behind with such baggage and records that could not be taken. Just before this date, Capt. R. D. T. McClintock, who had been mobilised with the unit, was posted for duty with the R. E., much to his personal regret, and the regret of the whole unit.

After a long night journey the Battalion detrained at Gourock, and at once embarked on board the *Duchess of Atholl,* which remained moored in mid-stream for two days before it sailed.

It was a pleasant voyage across the Atlantic to America, and was marked by an event which must have impressed itself very forcibly on the memories of those who witnessed it. Before arrival in America, what appeared to be a mighty fleet approached over the horizon which quite overshadowed the small British naval escort which had been in charge of the convoy during the early part of the voyage.

This fleet turned out to be part of the American Navy, which divided on meeting our ships and then turned inwards taking the place of our original escort which turned outwards and away, disappearing into the mists to the west.

As the convoy steamed up the estuary towards Halifax the early morning sun was rising and a good view of the harbour and town was obtained, but there was no chance of seeing the city of Halifax from closer quarters, for immediately on arrival at the docks, all personnel were transferred at once to other transports.

Within thirty-six hours the Division was again on its way and passing through the West Indies, reached Trinidad. A stop was made here for refuelling and to take on water, and then the convoy was once more at sea. No land was seen again until Cape Town was reached about three weeks later, when, after docking, all troops were allowed ashore.

The welcome given to the Division on arrival at Cape Town could not well have been greater, and the hospitality extended to each and every member was such that the four-and-a-half days in South Africa was a wonderful holiday to everyone. The arrangements made for the entertainment of the troops were so extensive that each individual was greeted personally by some local citizen or family.

After leaving Cape Town, the convoy steamed northwards and was approaching Bombay, when the ship in which were the 53rd Infantry Brigade, turned about and proceeded without escort towards Mombassa, which was reached by midday on 25th December. This was the third war Christmas for most of the unit.

Escorted by the cruiser *Emerald* the voyage across the Indian Ocean, and the year, closed with the arrival of the convoy at one of the Maldive Islands for refuelling and to take on water.

Escorted by the cruiser *Exeter,* the convoy moved towards Singapore, and on 13th January, 1942, the Battalion disembarked from USS *Mount Vernon* at the naval base on Singapore Island.

The Battalion structure at the time was as follows:

Battalion HQ:
LIEUT. COL. I. C. G. LYWOOD
MAJOR A. B. CUBITT
CAPT. P. J. HILL
CAPT. R. F. GRIFFITHS
CAPT. W. R. JACKSON, RAMC
LIEUT. QMR. H. G. CLARK
RSM C. LEVERIDGE
RQMS H. HENDREY

HQ Company:
CAPT. A. R. STACY
CAPT. R. R. EVANS
LIEUT. E. J. GODDARD
2ND LIEUT. R. O. C. GODDARD
2ND LIEUT. D. G. HORNER

'A' Company:
CAPT. P. S. CAMPBELL-ORDE
LIEUT. C. J. CALDER
LIEUT. A. W. NOCK
LIEUT. H. R. C. C. COOK
2ND LIEUT. G. A. KIDNER
CSM M. RUDLING
CQMS C. REEVE

'B' Company:
MAJOR J. M. SMYTH
CAPT. J. C. STRATFORD
LIEUT. R. R. W. GARRETT
2ND LIEUT. H. C. C. ROSS
2ND LIEUT. A. E. COX
CSM N. TWIDDY
CQMS L. SMITH

'C' Company:
CAPT. H. P. PILKINGTON
LIEUT. J. C. RACE
2ND LIEUT. J. B. KELF
2ND LIEUT. N. E. PARKER
2ND LIEUT. R. H. NUTT
CSM E. KELF

'D' Company:
CAPT. P. M. WESTGATE
LIEUT. R. T. F. DAYKIN
2ND LIEUT. F. T. C. OFFORD
2ND LIEUT. G. J. SMITH
2ND LIEUT. A. E. JONES
CSM C. LORD
CQMS S. HARDWICK

First Reinforcements:
MAJOR H. S. LING, MC
CAPT. D. P. APTHORP
LIEUT. J. L. MACKWOOD
2ND LIEUT. M. C. MITCHELL
2ND LIEUT. J. A. SALTER
2ND LIEUT. E. L. WEYMONT

Total Officers: 38
Total Other Ranks: 877
Battalion Strength: 915

A tropical rainstorm providentially prevented the convoy from being bombed at anchor by the Japanese planes which were heard passing overhead. However, the rain successfully soaked all personnel and their baggage during transit to Tyersall Park Camp, where the Battalion spent its first two days.

On the 16th January the Battalion embussed for the journey to the mainland of Malaya, leaving the first reinforcements at No. 7 M.R.C., the command of which had been taken over by Lieut. Col. H. S. Ling, MC. Four F.M.S.V.F. officers were attached for the interrogation of natives and to act as interpreters, and their services proved very useful during operations. It was thought at first that the Battalion was proceeding to the mainland for training in jungle warfare, and to get its 'land legs' after three months at sea. There was further indication that this was the idea when four Indian Army officers were appointed as instructors for this class of training. But this was not to be the case, and on arrival at Ayer Hitam, the Battalion was ordered to take up a defensive position astride the Muar-Yong Peng road on a ridge 10 miles south of Muar. The task was to cover the lines of communication of the 45th Infantry Brigade at Muar, who were being heavily attacked by the enemy, and to cover their possible withdrawal.

On 17th January the Battalion was in position supported by one troop of 4.5 howitzers, and on the next day had its baptism of fire in a dive-bombing attack by enemy aeroplanes on the forward companies, 'D' and 'C', and on Battalion H.Q. The position was in thick jungle save for the forward slopes of the ridge, with deep irrigation ditches and swamps at the sides of the road which made it extremely difficult to get vehicles under good cover and off the road.

On the 18th our patrols had contacted some Japanese patrols to the west, and later some Australians from two Battalions which had passed through the 6th Battalion lines to reinforce the 45th Infantry Brigade, reported that the Japanese had cut off the 43rd Infantry Brigade and attacked the Australian 'B' Echelon Transport some six miles to the north.

The next day the enemy attacked 'C' Company on the left from the jungle on the left (west) flank of the Battalion. They over-ran 'C' Company and managed to get astride the road on the top of the ridge behind 'D' Company The enemy were in considerable strength, and a counter-attack by one company Loyals, and 'B' Company was unsuccessful.

On the 20th January, the 3/16 Punjabis, having moved up by night, delivered a dawn attack on the ridge, but suffered severe casualties and were unsuccessful. A further attack by the Loyals was to have been launched the next day, but owing to the inaccuracy of the supporting artillery fire, it had to be called off. The Battalion was now in support of the other two Battalions of the Brigade covering a swamp over which the road passed. Lieut. Col. I. C. G. Lywood had been evacuated and Major A. B. Cubitt took over command of the Battalion which now consisted of 'A' and 'B' Companys and the remains of 'C' Company.

On the 23rd January this composite Brigade, under the command of Brigadier Duke, was ordered to withdraw to Yong Peng, eight miles to the south, commencing at midday with the 6th Battalion acting as rearguard. The enemy from his commanding position quickly followed up the withdrawal, and the Battalion was heavily engaged. Having successfully held off the enemy attacks until 1930 hours, the Battalion successfully broke off the engagement and withdrew to Yong Peng, and later moved to Skudi, south of Ayer Hitam, where it remained for one day.

On the night of the 24th/25th January, the Battalion moved to Sanggarang with Battalion H.Q. and 'B' Company, leaving 'A' Company at Rengit, nine miles south of Sanggarang. The Battalion was to hold the river crossings at both places in support of the 15th Infantry Brigade at Batu Pahat, nine miles to the north on the west coast of Malaya. The 15th Infantry Brigade was composed of the 5th Royal Norfolk, 2nd Cambridgeshire, and the 'British Battalion' (composed of the amalgamated Leicestershire and East Surrey regular Battalions), and this was the first occasion during the battle when other units of the 53rd Brigade were near at hand.

Information was received that there were no enemy south of Batu Pahat, but soon after dawn, on arrival at Sanggarang, the enemy attacked from the south, and established road blocks between Sanggarang and Rengit. A force composed of 6th Battalion reinforcements from Singapore, armoured cars, and a section of 4.5 howitzers and endeavoured unsuccessfully to clear the road blocks from Rengit and suffered very severe casualties. Rengit was attacked soon afterwards, and 'A' Company, having held off all the attacks, was ordered by Brigade H.Q. to withdraw to Benut by the jungle, which they accomplished very successfully.

On 27th January, 15th Infantry Brigade, on becoming acquainted with the situation in the south, withdrew to Sanggarang, and attempted to clear the enemy from the road blocks. By 1800 hours, as they had met with little success, the Brigade with the 6th Battalion now under command, were ordered to withdraw via the jungle independently by units and try to get back to Benut. The Battalion moved west of the road, and next day, in conjunction with the 'British Battalion', contacted some naval gunboats at the fishing village of Pongor on the west coast. Here reliable information was received that Benut had been captured by the enemy and the troops were therefore evacuated by sea on the gunboats to

Singapore. This took three nights and did not prove at all easy as the river used was very small with mangrove swamps on either side and the enemy were only one mile away on the main road.

At Singapore, the 53rd Infantry Brigade was reorganised and re-equipped, but though the remainder of the 18th Division had now arrived, it remained under command of the 11th Indian Division.

The British forces now having been evacuated from the Malayan mainland, the 53rd Brigade took up a position on the 3rd February on the north coast of Singapore Island from the naval base to the River Seletar. The 6th Battalion was on the right flank north of the River Seletar, and on the other side of the river were the 5th Battalion Beds and Herts of 55th Brigade 18th Division The Battalion now consisted of three companies: 'A', 'B' and 'C', men of 'D' Company, many of whom had managed to extricate themselves from the position at Yong Peng and got back to the Battalion via the jungle, being posted to the other companies to bring their strength nearer establishment. From this time until 12th February all ranks worked feverishly in the construction of defences, of which there were non on the arrival of the Battalion in that area. The work was done mostly at night as the enemy had good 'O.P.s' on the Johore side of the Straits opposite. The morale of the Battalion was now high, as at last the measure of jungle warfare had been taken, and coast defence was not a new experience. With defences prepared, the impending Japanese attack was waited for in confidence.

However, the Japanese attacked on the west coast of the Causeway, and on the 12th, after a succession of rumours of successes by the enemy, the brigade was ordered to withdraw as quickly as possible, as the enemy had all but gained possession of the bridge at Nee Soon, the only Battalion. The Battalion now covered the withdrawal of the Brigade over the Seletar, and took up a position at the seventh milestone on the naval base–Singapore road with the 2nd Cambridgeshire Regiment and 2/19 Australian Battalion. Next day, the enemy attacked strongly in the very thick jungle and managed to infiltrate through the defensive positions and at dawn on the 14th February the Battalion withdrew to a position on Braddell Road in reserve behind the 5th Battalion.

On the 15th February, orders were received at 1400 hours that hostilities would cease at 1600 hours that day. Later, information was received that the British forces had capitulated and that the Battalion was to concentrate in its present position and await orders. Thus ended the short campaign, and it is fair to say that the Battalion fought with considerable merit, especially as it had received no training in jungle warfare, and did not act as a Motorised Battalion, for which role the 18th Division had been training so long in England. The evacuation of casualties was carried out admirably, under extreme difficulties, by Capt. W. R. Jackson, R.A.M.C., the Battalion M.O., and Sergeant A. Branson was awarded the Military Medal for conspicuous gallantry in evacuating the wounded.

On 17th February, 1942, the Battalion marched to Changi Barracks on the east coast of the Island of Singapore, and then started the three-and-a-half years of life as prisoners-of-war.

Battalion disembarked at Singapore with a strength of 38 officers, 877 other ranks.

Casualties during campaign:

	Killed or missing	Wounded
Officers	13	2
W.O.	1	1
Other ranks	165	72
Total	179	75

Prisoners of War

General Percival surrenders to the Japanese 15th February 1942

The two days immediately after capitulation saw the three Battalions of the Royal Norfolk Regiment develop intense speculation as to the future. Efforts were made to clear up lose ends, contacting those who had been separated from the Battalions during the confused fighting on the island and many men collected what personal effects they could muster for the inevitable captivity that lay ahead.

The Battalions marched about 17 miles to Changi Barracks on the East Coast of Singapore Island. Some men, however, found transport hidden in rubber plantations and many men were relayed to Changi without interference from the Japanese, finally they joined the rest of the weary 18th Division in captivity.

The Barracks having escaped the serious bombing and shelling to which the rest of the island had been subjected, were consequently in excellent condition but there was no water or light, this was soon rectified by our Royal Engineers. There was however serious overcrowding and several huts had to be built. Many of the Norfolk's were crammed into the NAAFI of Roberts Barracks. The officers were in the Chinese coolies quarters, two and three officers in the space usually occupied by one Chinese.

Food was very scarce, practically no meat, rice being the main diet. This change in diet had an adverse effect, some soldiers couldn't go to the toilet for over 20 days!

Attempts were made to organise concerts to relieve the boredom of captivity and vegetable gardens were started whenever possible to supplement the meagre rations, also various forms of study and education for all ranks in the form af a "university".

It was also during Changi that a renegade Sikh Battalion mutinied and were put in charge, they put up road blocks, demanded stringent respect and made the situation even more difficult.

It was not long before dysentery became prevalent, one of the early deaths being the Padre, Capt. the Rev. J. O. Dean, whom all ranks were grieved to lose. In March work details were sent to Singapore. This was a relief, as small parties were sent out over the city and were able to get extra food and other necessities. Large quantities of books were also acquired by various means.

By the end of April men were marched to Singapore and accommodated in tents in Farrar Park Camp. Here food improved considerably. Also some pay was issued to those who worked, about 25 cents a day, the equivalent of about 4d., so that a little extra food, especially bananas and pineapples could be bought. It was often possible to steal food from the Japanese, and other items which were sold to the Chinese. One amusing thing happened during this time. A party of men got some flour as they thought from the docks but when they made some dumplings they set as hard as bricks, the supposed flour being plaster of Paris.

During this period there were practically no medical supplies, but the health of the Battalion remained good. As an example of the Japanese mentality, a Japanese store was raided one night by a party of Malays and some were killed in the ensuing fight. The heads of these were put up in about eight prominent places such as the railway station, etc.

During the Summer, everyone was forced to sign a declaration saying that he would not escape. At first this was refused, and all prisoners of war in Changi were ordered to Selerang Barracks.

Prisoners held in the southern area of Singapore had to travel the furthest, approximately 2 miles over steep hills to Selerang. The Norfolks, the rest of the 18th Division and the 11th Division were closer, and the Australians were already being held at the barracks. The two roads connecting with Selerang were soon covered with troops, many in teams pushing trailers, handcarts, even wheelbarrows, piled dangerously high with rations, cooking stoves, fuel, utensils and bedding. It was also pathetic to see lads just managing to get along. Lads who were beri-beri cases, amputation cases, struggling along on crutches and for so many reasons men, who could only just walk - but all determined to get there somehow! Some men took over four hours to cover one mile. Spirits were kept high, after struggling to the top of a hill men would simply laugh and joke and the cries like: 'Off to Brighton for the weekend!' were heard.

All these men were crammed into a barracks built for *one Battalion* of British Infantry. After a couple of days all supplies, including those for medical needs, were cut. Diphtheria and dysentery became epidemic and nobody was allowed to be

The rice ration is issued at Kanchanaburi

removed to hospital - one man had to be operated on for appendicitis. In these dire conditions the British Commander ordered all ranks to sign the declaration saying of course that, as it was done under pressure, it had no meaning. The men, having now pacified their captors, were allowed to trek back to their original camps.

The senior British and Australian Commanders were made to witness the shooting of two British and two Australian soldiers who had previously attempted to escape. It has since been seen in the press that the Japanese General responsible was himself sentenced to be shot, and the sentence was carried out in the same place. Great help was given to the Battalion by many Eurasian and Chinese. Such help included gifts of food, medical supplies, musical instruments and, later, wireless parts. The Japanese camp Commander in Farrar Park most of this time was a sergeant by the name of Asouki who did a great deal to help.

A railway was ordered by the Japanese High Command to support their troops deep into Burma and Siam. It was to be built in 18 months, however this order was counter-commandered and construction was to be completed in one year – which it was at a horrific cost in life. At this point to recount the experiences of the three Battalions as bodies of the Royal Norfolk Regiment becomes difficult because men from all Battalions in captivity made up the railway work parties which were constantly demanded. Laterly even very sick men were sent from Singapore up country to work during 'Speedo'. Notably 'F' and 'H' forces which consisted of large numbers of Norfolk men experienced tremendous hardships and casualties.

Towards the end of June the camp at Changi began to split up. The first party to go was from the 6th Battalion, under the command of Capt. Goddard, and its destination was Thailand, where it was to assist in building a railway. At the time of its departure it was rather envied by those left behind. None as yet knew what that railway was to cost in human life and suffering.

In September, 1942, the 5th Battalion was moved to Serangoon Road, a mile away. This camp was being rebuilt. The accommodation consisted of palm leaf huts. The men had to sleep in very crowded conditions on wooden platforms in two tiers, which soon became very full of bed bugs. This camp was 2,000 strong and commanded by a Japanese officer. The guards were now changed from fighting soldiers to

A member of the Kempetai (Secret Police), executed after the war for atrocities committed against Prisoners of War

Prisoner of War guards who were Koreans with Japanese N.C.O.'s and were all a very bad lot. Lieut. Col. Prattley was Camp Commander. One evening he was badly beaten over the back with a rifle by a drunken Japanese L.Cpl. In September, the officers at last got a little pay, about $10 a month. The British Commander laid down certain contributions towards men's messing and hospital upkeep. A good concert party and band were now gradually forming. Also a few selected canteen suppliers were allowed into the camp once a week. Eventually electric light and shower baths were erected. In October, a Red Cross ship was allowed in, and a very welcome issue of clothes and medical stores, food and cigarettes was made.

It was also in October that the move to Thailand was accelerated. Further parties were ordered there, including a large one from the 4th Battalion under Lieut. Col. Knights, others leaving for destinations in Burma, Indo-China, Formosa, the Philippines and Japan. It was impossible to keep a check on all men in the three Battalions as they

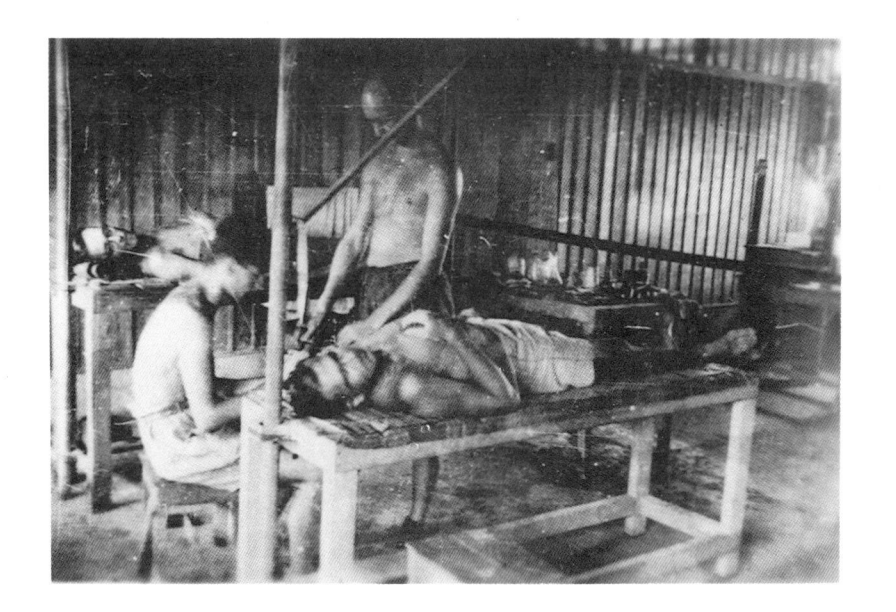

Blood donors at Temuang. This picture shows the primitive medical conditions. With no issue of medical supplies by the Japanese anaesthetic was a luxury when it could be "aquired". Many medical instruments were improvised or made out of scrap found around the camp. Many operations were carried out with Gillette razor blades and the doctors were indefatigable.

became split up a factor which caused many regrets among both officers and men.

After Christmas the 5th Battalion moved back to Changi and were accommodated in a barrack room block in Roberts Barracks. There was much more room after the working groups were despatched.

Some really good concerts and plays were carried out in Changi. During this period of captivity, the Battalion Medical Officer was Capt. Chopping, R.A.M.C., who, apart from being a very good doctor, was also a wireless expert, and had made, in Singapore, a very fine compact wireless set, so that there was no lack of news from the outside world.

As 1943 progressed more and more men were shunted up into Thailand for work on the railway, only the sick and wounded remaining in Singapore.

On the 18th March, 1943, a party of 550 other ranks (400 5th Battalion and 150 6th Battalion) and five officers, Major Crane, Capt. Hammond, Capt. Self, Lieut. Curtis, Lieut. Battersby were ordered to go to Siam to work on the railway which was being made from Bangkok to Rangoon. The party was taken by M.T. to Singapore and then put into steel goods wagons, 25 plus kit to a wagon. This railway was metre gauge, so the overcrowding and heat turned the wagons into ovens. The journey took five days and the men had two meals a day, chiefly rice. By the time the men arrived at Non Pradok they were completely exhausted.

The Japanese issued five unripe bananas per man and a close-by Prisoner of War Camp was able to provide tea. The party was moved into another train of open trucks, 50 men were put in each truck and were wedged like sardines in a tin.

The track was very uneven and the train proceeded very slowly at 5-10 miles per hour, which was not enough to make a cool draught. It was blazing hot, which was not made any better when the train stopped for about an hour and a half at noon whilst the guards went and had a meal. No prisoners were allowed to leave the trucks.

The party arrived at Kanburi and were marched one mile and ordered into the jungle. This had to be cleared and everyone bivouacked in the open. Just before dark, rations were delivered which were very much better than had ever been issued before, rice, vegetables, pork and eggs. The great difficulty was cooking as the Japanese would not allow any cooking pots to be taken from Singapore, and only a very few were issued. The next day working parties had to be found to work on the railway. Troops were allowed to bathe in the river about a mile away. In the evenings it rained and everyone got soaking wet. It was not until after about eight days that some tents and tarpaulins were issued. In the meantime, further parties from Singapore arrived daily until there were about 5,000 troops in the area. On about the 3rd April, 1943, the party was ordered to move on again. It was transported by the trolleys which carried the rails for laying and were drawn by diesel rail cars which could also be converted for road use. About 50 men were left behind suffering from malaria and dysentery, and these were moved to the base hospital nearby, run by a British Medical Officer and Staff.

This journey was not too bad as the trucks went faster and the day was cooler. In the evening the party was detrained at Wompo which was then the rail head, further progress being stopped by a viaduct which had to be quarried out of a cliff face. Five tents, each about 14 ft. by 18 ft. were issued and a camp was made on the river bank. The following day work was started from daylight till dark. One party had to work for 24 hours on end. The guards here were Koreans. Beatings by guards and Japanese Railway engineers were frequent. No pay had been issued since leaving Singapore until the last evening in this camp. The pay issued in Singapore was no use in Siam as it took three months to get this changed.

On about 14th April, the party had to march about 10 miles to Tarso, and about another 50 men were left behind for evacuation to base hospital. No transport of any sort was provided and everything had to be carried. This was a very hard march. The stay in Tarso was only for a few days; again men were just put into a jungle clearing without cover. On about 17th April, the party started to move by M.T. in three lifts, one going each day, to Takanun. In this, the party was very lucky because every subsequent party had to march about 90 miles.

On arrival at Takanun, tents were issued on a scale of one per 25 men. All ranks were made to work on the railway and also on a Japanese camp. No men were allowed to build a cook house or dig latrines. The food was very bad, practically rice only. The camp was situated on the river bank with the trace of the railway on the other side. The surrounding jungle was of very dense prickly bamboo and practically impenetrable. More parties started to arrive and pass through the camp daily. Meanwhile the hard work, exposure, lack of proper food and medical supplies began to tell on everyone. The two Medical Officers with the party, Capts. Donaldson and Petrovisky, R.A.M.C., did wonderful work with what little medicine they had. When the monsoon broke at the end of May, conditions became terrible as the tents were made of very poor quality material and not only did they not keep the wet out but became completely rotten after about one month. Cholera hit the camp causing a great many deaths. Not for some time did the Japanese allow the camp to build any hospital huts to cope with the growing number of sick men with other ailments such as bronchitis, beri-beri, malaria, amoebic dysentery and diphtheria.

All the fit men of the camp were moved to another camp a short distance away. Lieut. Battersby was in command of the fit men of the Norfolk party of about 100 men. Capt. Hamond and Capt. Self both had cholera but managed to get over it successfully. It was several days before the Japanese would allow any sick to be evacuated to base hospitals. This was a long journey by barge. Altogether during this period, the party had about 170 deaths.

We must also remember the constant abuse and torture of prisoners took a horrific toll. The work was murderously hard. In places the railway ran through rocky hills, here the track had to be levelled by hand with crowbars and sledge

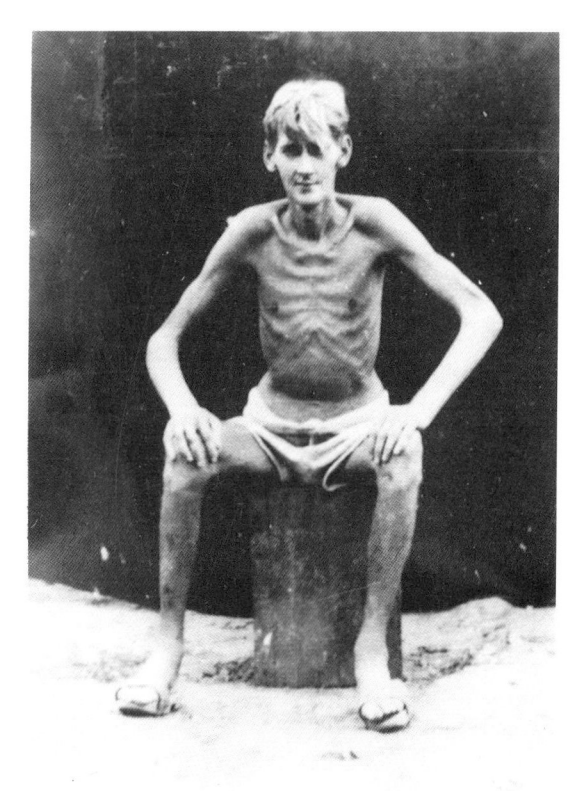

A chronic case of malnutrition, all too common among the prisoners.

hammers. The tools provided for the work were primitive in the extreme adding to the labours of the construction.

So the work went on and the 'Railway of Death' pursued its way into the jungle - for every sleeper laid a British, Australian or Dutch life was taken (about 13,000) and countless thousands of coolies from Malaya.

In effect most of the Norfolks' role in completion of the railway was done by October 1943. Conditions became much better and huts were built of bamboo and palm leaf. Parties were organised to work in the cemetery and a stage was built, and food also improved considerably. During that winter it used to be very heartening to hear our bombers fly overhead at night on their way to and from objectives such as Bangkok, Saigon, etc.

Quite a good amount of food was available for Christmas, and all ranks had a riceless day and a pantomime in the evening.

In February, all fit men were organised to go to Japan. No officers of the 5th Battalion were allowed or detailed to go by the Japanese. A R.S.M. Spencer was in command of the Norfolk men in this party.

Early in March 1944, Takanun camp was evacuated and everyone was moved by rail down towards Bangkok to a base camp at Chunki. This was a large camp accommodating about 11,000 Prisoners of War. The place was very well organised although everything was improvised as the Japanese supplied nothing. There were tailors, boot-makers, laundry, theatre and band, good cookhouses and canteens. The hospital, although it had very little equipment and practically no medical supplies, did wonderful work. The cemetery at that time was looked after by senior officers and was very well laid out in grass and tropical flowering shrubs.

Men evacuated sick from up country working parties were, when discharged from hospital,

Prisoners of War recuperating in Changi Jail, Singapore, 1945

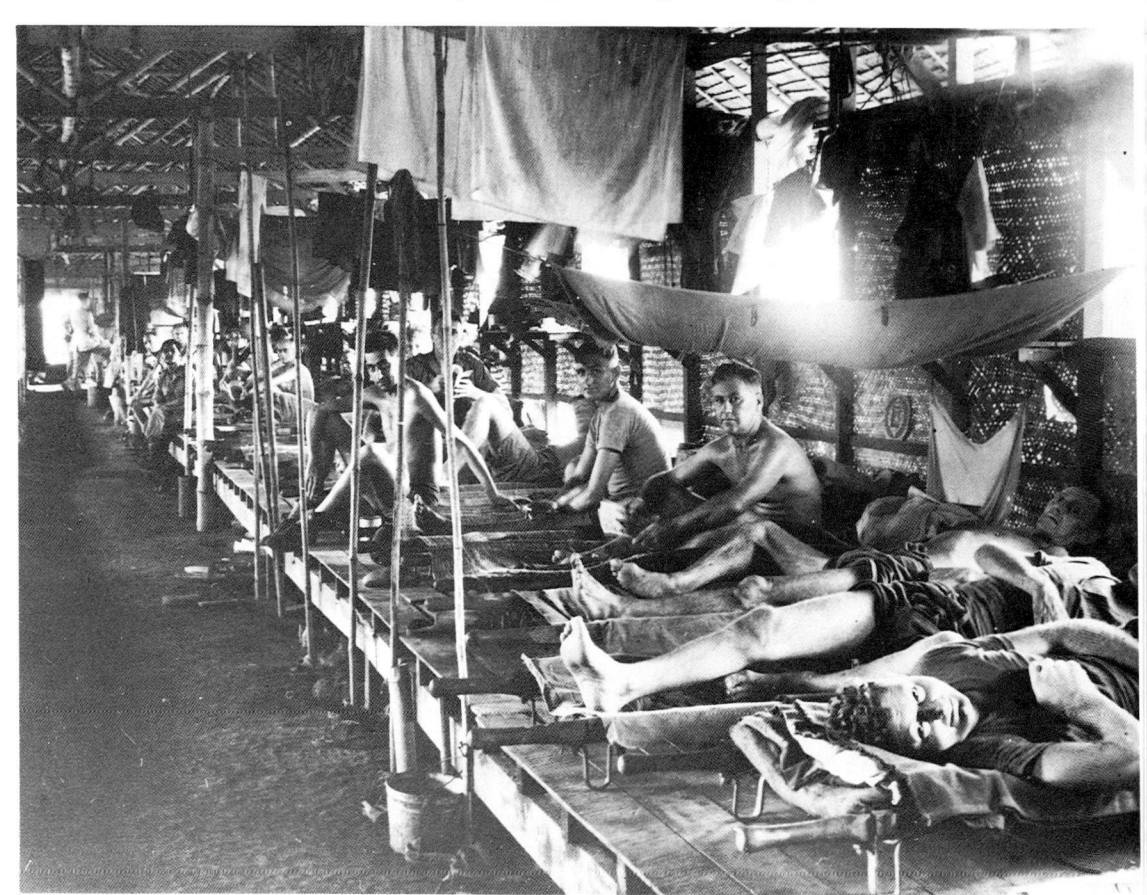

Men of the 4th, 5th and 6th Battalions at Aomi Hall, Japan, 1945

taken into a combined Norfolk Battalion commanded by Lieut. Col. A. B. Cubitt. In May, working parties were sent up country again for railway maintenance and firewood cutting for the locomotives. During the monsoon, owing to washouts and bombing, the railway did not operate at all efficiently. In the Summer, some American Red Cross parcels arrived and were distributed; about six men shared a parcel. Some other camps did not get any as the Japanese took them for themselves. At the same time quite a good amount of medical stores also came. These were very much needed and must have saved many lives.

In November, twenty-one Liberators flew low over the camp. The fact of seeing our own bombers flying low overhead put all ranks in very good heart. The bombers dropped some bombs on a bridge some three moles away. Unfortunately some bombs went into Tamakan camp close to the bridge and caused some casualties. This camp was later evacuated and the bridge, a big girder one on concrete piles was later completely destroyed by allied bombers. Christmas was spent at Chunki in much the same way as previously.

In February 1945, all officers were taken away from the men and put in Kanburi camp about six miles away. When the end came the Battalion was scattered in small parties on different parts of the railway. These parties were taken to either Bangkok or Petburi aerodromes and as they arrived were flown to Rangoon.

Petburi aerodrome was built by Prisoners of War and the first planes to use it were our Dakotas sent by the Americans who were magnificent evacuating the camp in the monsoon.

The end came with dramatic suddenness. It had been known from the camp wireless sets that Germany had gone down to total defeat in May of 1945, and all realised that the Allies would now concentrate the whole of their energies on the Far Eastern war, and that the days of Japan were numbered. By early August there was a distinct change in the attitude of the Japanese prison guards, and their former brutality changed to a cringing servility. On August 15th all camps were buzzing with rumours and it could hardly be believed that Japan had surrendered. But within a few days, relieving officers and supplies from Burma were parachuted on to the camps, to bring vivid reality to the fact of freedom. Gradually all prisoners were brought down to centres where they could be re-equipped with clothing and properly housed, preparatory to a return to England. The long months of captivity had at last came to an end.

In spite of all the Japanese could do, the brutality of guards, frequent beatings, humiliation and torture suffered, the men of the 4th, 5th and 6th Battalions of the Royal Norfolk Regiment never forgot they were soldiers. It was their steady discipline, inflexible courage through adversity and a native dignity and comradeship unique to Norfolk men that brought them through their horrific ordeal.

A triumph through death and disablement, may they never be forgotten and those of us who are left with their legacy 'keep going the spirit that kept them going'.

Returned home, men representing all Battalions of the Royal Norfolk Regiment formed this detachment under Major H. R. Holden, MC, to escort the Colours on the Victory Day march through London, June 1946

Telephone
Norwich 22233.

The Lord Mayor's Parlour,
City Hall,
Norwich.

December 7th, 1945.

My dear Sir,

It is with much pleasure that I am able to write to you now that you have returned to the City after undergoing the privations of being a prisoner of war in Japanese hands. Now that most of the ex-prisoners of war have returned from the war East it is felt the time is opportune for the Corporation to invite them to an informal dinner and entertainment at which I shall be able to offer them a civic welcome.

This dinner and entertainment will be held in St. Andrew's Hall on Thursday, 3rd January, 1946, at 6.30 for 6.45 p.m. I enclose a stamped addressed postcard to my Secretary which I shall be glad if you will fill in and post. All you need do is to cross out one of the two lines stating whether you do or you do not propose to be present and add your name, rank, regiment and address at the bottom of the postcard.

This letter in itself does not admit you, but those accepting this invitation will receive a few days before the 3rd January a booklet containing the menu of the dinner and particulars of the Concert which will be the admission ticket. Persons accepting the invitation will enter by the Blackfriars' Hall door at the corner of St. Andrew's Hall Plain. Blackfriars' Hall will be used for the purpose of a cloakroom.

I shall be glad to receive an early reply stating whether or not you are able to be present so that the necessary arrangements for the dinner can be put in hand at once.

Yours very truly,

S. A. Bailey
Lord Mayor.

C.S.M. M. McGrory,
58, Ketts Hill,
NORWICH.

Letter sent to returned Norwich FEPOWs

BUCKINGHAM PALACE

The Queen and I bid you a very warm welcome home.

Through all the great trials and sufferings which you have undergone at the hands of the Japanese, you and your comrades have been constantly in our thoughts. We know from the accounts we have already received how heavy those sufferings have been. We know also that these have been endured by you with the highest courage.

We mourn with you the deaths of so many of your gallant comrades.

With all our hearts, we hope that your return from captivity will bring you and your families a full measure of happiness, which you may long enjoy together.

George R.I.

September 1945.

Certificate sent to all returned FEPOWs